C-ELNS 781

C-ELNS 781

A CATALOGUE OF BOOKBINDINGS

Nicholas T. Smith

Publisher

Bronxville, New York

Of this Catalogue three hundred copies have
been printed in 1979 for Nicholas T. Smith, Publisher
at the Town House Press, Spring Valley, New York

This is Copy Number ___________________

A CATALOGUE OF BOOKS BOUND BY S. T. PRIDEAUX BETWEEN MDCCCXC AND MDCCCC WITH TWENTY-SIX ILLUSTRATIONS

37 NORFOLK SQUARE LONDON

Library of Congress Catalogue Card Number 79-90681
International Standard Book Number: 0-935164-02-2

Printed in the United States of America

Nicholas T. Smith
Box 66
Bronxville, New York 10708

PREFACE

In putting forth the illuſtrations that accompany
this record of work, I feel prompted to ſay a few
words about deſign in its application to bindings.
They muſt not be taken as intending to lay down
rules of univerſal application, nor as implying
adverſe criticiſm of work executed upon radically
different methods, but rather as explanatory of
the illuſtrations themſelves. The iſſue of ſuch a
catalogue is in itſelf egotiſtical, & to be conſiſtent
throughout I ſhall deſcribe the lines on which I
have endeavoured to decorate my covers, lines
that have naturally become clearer to me with
the continued effort of achievement. I ſay ' endeavoured' with much meaning, for endeavour
and realiſation are two very different things, and
no one is more conſcious than I that in the illuſtrations given there is a good deal more of the
firſt than of the laſt.
This may at any rate be conceded ; that thoſe of
us intereſted in the return to life of any art that
has ſuccumbed to the deadening influence of mere
convention, attempt in that art what gives moſt
pleaſure to ourſelves and not what public taſte
demands.
Perſonally, I like decoration at all times uſed with
great reſerve, and ſtrictly confined to very limited

I

proportions. It gives me but little pleasure to see a book covered with a mass of small ' tooling ' which effectually hides the beauty of the underlying material, and necessitates much study before the design can be distinguished. What is the use of selecting at great cost of money and time the finest & most flawless skins only to overlay them with a glitter of gold ? To use inferior material, & in this way conceal its defects, has long been the device of the cheap bookbinder. When once we have learnt to appreciate the quality of skins we realise that hardly out of France may be found a book habited in the very best : much of the very costly and most decorated work turned out by our chief binders is put upon morocco that would only be used in France for what is contemptuously described as ' de la camelote '.

It seems perhaps the language of exaggeration to speak of the architectural qualities of design, especially when design is on such a small scale as must of necessity be the case when applied to bindings. But the fact remains that it is difficult to find another word that tersely expresses the qualities of simplicity of proportion and dignity of line, unobscured by a burden of detail.

It appears to me essential that the main lines of any design should be of this character. We may say indeed that it should be seen at once whence

they come and whither they go, and that they
ſhould not be tortured into the myſtery of a puzzle.
This was obviouſly held as a truth by the early
Italian binders, and by French binders alſo before
the advent of the Eves. Up to this time French
bindings are bold and fine in deſign ; they have a
certain reſtraint in their freedom, a certain ſim-
plicity in their elaboration that marks the higheſt
point ever attained. Notwithſtanding its ſumptu-
ouſneſs the exceſſive floriated detail of the Eves
together with their multiplication of the parts of
a deſign indicates in my opinion the decadence of
the art. To the great admiration beſtowed upon
the Eve books in our time is, no doubt, largely due
the trivial over-decoration of much of the work
appreciated both here and in America.
A deſign ſhould then, I think, be eaſily read in
its main conſtruction, without of courſe being too
obvious. But the problem of attaining the golden
mean is not more difficult for the binder than for
the proſe writer who has to avoid platitude on the
one hand and undue ſubtlety on the other. It fol-
lows upon this appreciation of the paramount
importance of line and breadth of effect that the
moſt ſuitable ſchemes for decorating a binding
ſhould be thoſe that utiliſe its natural lines and
inſiſt upon its rectangular and parallel character.
Hence as a ſcheme of decoration the border and

the panel come firſt in my eſtimate of appropri-
atenefs, and I own to a feeling of difcomfort when
I fee a defign that intentionally and obviouſly
runs counter to that chara&ter. 'All over' patterns
are occafionally pleafant in their total effe&t of
glitter and lavifhnefs, but are infinitely eafier to
make than the border or the panel. They do away
moreover with thofe untouched fpaces of leather
which befides fhowing the quality of the fkin,
give fo much value to the defign itſelf.
I notice a fallacy conftantly expreffed in criticifm
of bindings, (efpecially in America, where there
is more genuine love and difcuffion of the craft
than in England), namely that there is lefs ex-
penditure of labour in the making of an appar-
ently fimple defign than there is in one that feems
to be very elaborate. There cannot be a greater
miftake. It is, for example, comparatively eafy to
make a diaper pattern capable of endlefs repeti-
tion, while to make a pattern felf-contained within
a given fpace where the lines are few and ftruc-
tural may coft infinite time, thought and labour
before it is brought to any fatisfa&tory refult.
There is a feeling almoft always prefent, even
when not expreffed, and which will die hard if it
ever dies, that quantity as well as quality is an
effential fa&tor in fuccefsful ornament. Baldnefs
is not of neceffity fimplicity, nor is plainnefs of

neceffity beauty. Yet the truth remains that it
takes a great artift to make a thing at once fimple
and beautiful, and that though few attain that
ideal, it is neverthelefs a counfel of perfection to
thofe who ftrive.

Thefe then are the thoughts that have occurred
to me in my attempts at pattern making, and I
can only hope that the reader will not at once
turn to the illuftrations in expectation of finding
them adequately tranflated into fact. The illuftrations are felected to fhow different fchemes on
which effort has been bafed, and I fhall be fatif-
fied if, in even a few among them, may be found
the principles which they fo imperfectly try to
embody.

S. T. PRIDEAUX

5

NOTE

I offer this record of the books I have bound during the laſt ten years to my friends in England and America. It is their appreciation and encouragement that have enabled me, in the face of many difficulties, to continue work, the ſhortcomings of which I have always fully realiſed.

S. T. P.

CATALOGUE OF BOOKS BOUND BETWEEN MDCCCXC & MDCCCC

ARNOLD, MATTHEW. Selected Poems. Macmillan and Co. London 1893 Duodecimo. Golden Treaſury Series. Two copies.

AUCASSIN AND NICOLETE. Done into Engliſh by Andrew Lang. Publiſhed by David Nutt in the Strand 1887 Foolſcap Octavo.

AUCASSIN AND NICOLETTE. A Love Story. Edited & Tranſlated by F. W. Bourdillon. French and Engliſh. Kegan Paul & Co. London 1887 Octavo. Three copies.

AURELIUS ANTONINUS, MARCUS. The Thoughts of the Emperor Marcus Aurelius. Kegan Paul and Co. London 1890 Octavo. Parchment Series. Large paper.

BEECHING, HENRY CHARLES. Love's Looking Glaſs: a volume of poems [by H. C. B., J. W. Mackail and J. B. B. Nichols]. Percival and Co. London 1891 Octavo.

BLUNT, WILFRID SCAWEN. The Love Sonnets of Proteus. Kegan Paul and Co. London 1885 Octodecimo.

BROWNING, ROBERT. Sordello. E. Moxon. London 1840 Octavo.

BRIDGES, ROBERT SEYMOUR. Eros and Pſyche: a poem in twelve meaſures. The ſtory done into Engliſh from Apuleius. George Bell and Sons. London 1885 Octavo.

BRIDGES, R. S. The Shorter Poems of. George Bell & Sons. London 1890 Duodecimo. Six copies.

BRIDGES, R. S. John Keats, a critical eſſay with portrait. Privately printed. [Lawrence & Bullen] London 1895 Octavo. Two copies.

BULLEN, ARTHUR HENRY. Lyrics from the Dramatiſts of the Elizabethan Age. Lawrence and Bullen. London 1891 Octavo.

BULLEN, ARTHUR HENRY. Lyrics from the Song Books of the Elizabethan Age. Lawrence and Bullen. London 1891 Octavo.

CATULLUS. Attis in Engliſh Verſe with Diſ-ſertations by Grant Allen. D. Nutt. London 1892 Octavo. Two copies.

CALDECOTT, R. The Owls of Olynn Belfry. A tale. Illuſtrated by R. Caldecott. Field & Tuer. London 1886 Sextodecimo. Two copies.

DE IMITATIONE CHRISTI. Libri Quatuor. Of the Imitation of Chriſt. Four Books. Kegan Paul, Trench, Trübner & Co. Limited. London 1892 Octavo. Two copies.

DANIEL PRESS PUBLICATIONS.
BINYON, R. LAURENCE. Poems. Oxford
1895 Quarto. Two copies.

BOURDILLON, FRANCIS W. Ailes d'Alou-
ette. Oxford 1890 Quarto. Three copies.

BRIDGES, ROBERT. Hymns from the Yat-
tendon Hymnal. 1899 Quarto. Three copies.

FILIPPI, ROSINA. Three Japaneſe Plays for
Children. Illuſtrated by Alfred Parſons. Oxford
1897 Octavo. Two copies.

HERRICK, ROBERT. His Flowers. Oxford
1891 Octodecimo. Two copies.

KEATS, JOHN. Odes, Sonnets and Lyrics with
portrait. Oxford 1895 Quarto. Two copies.

WOODS, MARGARET L. Songs. Oxford
1896 Octavo. Four copies.

GRAHAME, KENNETH. The Golden Age.
John Lane. London 1895 Octavo.

HERRICK, ROBERT. The Heſperides and
Noble Numbers: edited by Alfred Pollard with a
preface by A. C. Swinburne. Two volumes. Lawrence and Bullen. London 1891 Octavo. Muſes
Library.

HOWELLS, WILLIAM DEAN. Their Wed-
ding Journey, with illuſtrations by C. Carleton.

Houghton and Mifflin. Boſton and New York
1895 Octavo.
HAFIZ, SHIRAZI. Ghazels from the Divan of
Hafiz. Done into Engliſh by J. H. McCarthy.
D. Nutt. London 1893 Octavo.
HENLEY, WILLIAM ERNEST. A Book of
Verſes. D. Nutt. London 1888 Octavo. Three
copies.
JACOBI, CHARLES THOMAS. Geſta Typo-
graphica, or a medley for printers and others. El-
kin Mathews. London 1897 Octavo.
KEATS, JOHN. Poems of. Macmillan and Co.
London 1894 Octavo. Golden Treaſury Series.
KEATS, JOHN. The Sonnets of. G. Bell and
Sons. London 1898. Duodecimo.

KELMSCOTT PRESS PUBLICATIONS.
MORRIS, WILLIAM. The Tale of King Flo-
rus and the Fair Jehane. Done out of ancient
French by William Morris. In black and red with
borders & woodcut title. 1893 Sextodecimo. Two
copies.
MORRIS, WILLIAM. Gothic Architecture.
A lecture for the Arts and Crafts Exhibition So-
ciety. With ornamental initials. 1893 Sexto-
decimo. Four copies.
MORRIS, WILLIAM. Of the Friendſhip of
Amis and Amile. Done out of ancient French, by

William Morris. In black and red with borders &
woodcut title. 1894 Sextodecimo. Five copies.
MORRIS, WILLIAM. The Tale of the Emperor Couſtans and of Over Sea. Done out of ancient French by William Morris. In black & red with borders & woodcut title. 1894 Sextodecimo. Two copies.
MORRIS, WILLIAM. Pſalmi Penitentiales: an Engliſh rhymed verſion of the Seven Penitential Pſalms. In black & red with ornamental borders and initials. 1894 Octavo. Two copies.
MORRIS, WILLIAM, Child Chriſtopher and Goldilind the Fair. In black and red with borders and woodcut title. Two Volumes. 1895 Sexto-decimo. Three copies.
SYR PERCYVELLE OF GALES. In black and red with borders and a woodcut deſigned by Sir E. Burne-Jones. 1895 Octavo.
SIRE DEGREVAUNT. In black and red with borders and a woodcut deſigned by Sir E. Burne-Jones. 1896 Octavo.
SYR YSAMBRACE. In black and red with borders and a woodcut deſigned by Sir E. Burne-Jones. 1897 Octavo.
Theſe three romances were reprinted from the Camden Society's volume of 1844.

THE FLOURE AND THE LEAFE and the
Boke of Cupide, God of Love, or the Cuckoo
& the Nightingale. In black and red with ornamental initials. 1896 Quarto. Three copies.
SPENSER, EDMUND. The Shepheardes Ca-
lendar, conteyning twelve Aeglogues proportion-
able to the twelve Moneths, with twelve illuſtrations by Arthur J. Gaſkin.In black and red. 1896
Quarto.

KINGSLEY, CHARLES. The Water-Babies,
with illuſtrations by Linley Sambourne. Mac-
millan and Co. London 1886 Octavo.
LANG, ANDREW. Ballads of Books. Edited
by A. L. [A recaſt of Ballads of Books edited by
Brander Matthews.] Longmans and Co. London
1888 Octavo.
LANG, ANDREW. Graſs of Parnaſſus. Long-
mans and Co. London 1888 Octavo.Five copies.
LANG, ANDREW. Helen of Troy. Bell and
Sons. London 1882 Octavo.
LANG, ANDREW. Letters on Literature.
Longmans and Co. London 1889 Octavo.
LANG, ANDREW. Ballads and Lyrics of Old
France with other Poems. 1896 Narrow foolſcap
octavo. Two copies.

LEFROY, EDWARD CRACROFT. Echoes from Theocritus. E.Stock. London 1885 Octavo.

LEVY, AMY. A London Plane Tree & A Minor Poet. T. Fiſher Unwin. London 1889 and 1891 Octavo. Cameo Series. Two copies.

LOVE IN IDLENESS. A volume of poems [by H. C. Beeching, J. W. Mackail, & J. B. B. Nichols.] Kegan Paul & Co. London 1883 Octavo. Two copies.

MORRIS, WILLIAM. The Defence of Guenevere, and other poems. Bell & Daldy. London 1858 Octavo. Three copies.

MORRIS, WILLIAM. The Defence of Guenevere. A book of Lyrics choſen from the works of William Morris. 1896 Narrow octavo.

OMAR KHAYYAM. Rubáiyát of Omar Kháyyám. Rendered into Engliſh verſe by E. Fitzgerald. Macmillan and Co. London 1890 Octavo. Four copies.

OMAR KHAYYAM. Rubáiyát of Omar Kháyyám, tranſlated by J. H. McCarthy, M.P. D. Nutt. London 1889 Octavo.

PEMBER, E. H. The Voyage of the Phocæans and other poems with the Prometheus Bound of Aeſchylus done into Engliſh verſe by E.H.P. Printed at the Chiſwick Preſs for private diſtribution. London 1895.

PEMBER, E. H. Adraſtus of Phrygia & other poems with the Hippolytus of Euripides done into Engliſh verſe by E.H.P. Printed at the Chiſwick Preſs for private diſtribution. London 1897.

PEMBER, E. H. Debita Flacco : echoes of ode and epode. Printed at the Chiſwick Preſs for private diſtribution. London 1891.

PRIDEAUX, S. T. Hiſtorical Sketch of Bookbinding with a chapter on early ſtamped bindings by E. G. Duff [and a bibliography.] Lawrence and Bullen. London 1893 Octavo. Fifteen copies.

ROSSETTI, DANTE GABRIEL. The Houſe of Life; a Sonnet Sequence for the firſt time given in its full text. Copeland and Day. Boſton 1894 Quarto. Two copies.

SAPPHO. Memoir, text, ſelected renderings and literal tranſlation by H. T. Wharton. Greek and Engliſh. John Lane. London 1895 Octavo. Three copies.

SCOTT, SIR WALTER. The Lyrics and Ballads of Sir Walter Scott: edited with an introduction by Andrew Lang. J. M. Dent and Co. London 1894 Octavo.

SHAKESPEARE, WILLIAM. Songs &

Sonnets: edited by F. T. Palgrave. Macmillan. London 1865 Sextodecimo. Gem edition.

SHELLEY, PERCY BYSSHE. The Cenci: a Tragedy in five acts [& in verſe] Italy. Printed for C. & J. Ollier. Vere Street London 1819 Octavo.

SHELLEY, PERCY BYSSHE. Select Letters: edited with an introduction by R. Garnett. Kegan Paul & Co. London 1882 Octavo.

STRETTELL, ALMA. Spaniſh and Italian Folk-Songs. Tranſlated by Alma Strettell, with photogravures. Macmillan and Co. London 1887 Octavo. Two copies.

STEVENSON, ROBERT LOUIS. A Child's Garden of Verſes. Longmans and Co. London 1885 Sextodecimo. Two copies.

STEVENSON, ROBERT LOUIS. An Inland Voyage. Kegan Paul and Co. London 1878.

STEVENSON, ROBERT LOUIS. Travels with a Donkey in the Cevennes. Kegan Paul and Co. London 1879 Octavo.

STEVENSON, ROBERT LOUIS. Underwoods. Chatto and Windus. London 1887 Octavo. Six copies.

STEVENSON, ROBERT LOUIS. Virginibus Pueriſque. Kegan Paul and Co. London 1881 Octavo. Two copies.

STEVENSON, ROBERT LOUIS. Virginibus Puerifque. Chatto and Windus. London 1887 Octavo. Two copies.

STEVENSON, ROBERT LOUIS. Memories and Portraits. Chatto and Windus. London 1887 Octavo. Two copies.

SWINBURNE, ALGERNON CHARLES. Atalanta in Calydon. Chatto and Windus. London 1882 Octavo.

SWINBURNE, ALGERNON CHARLES. Triftram of Lyoneffe and other poems. Chatto and Windus. London 1882 Octavo.

SYMONDS, JOHN ADDINGTON. Wine, Women and Song. Mediæval Latin Students' Songs. Chatto & Windus. London 1884 Octavo.

TABLEY, LORD DE. Poems Dramatic and Lyrical. Illuftrated by C. Ricketts. Firft Series. J. Lane. London 1893 Octavo.

TABLEY, LORD DE. Poems Dramatic and Lyrical. Illuftrated by C. Ricketts. Second Series. J. Lane. London 1895 Octavo.

UZANNE, OCTAVE. Bouquiniftes et Bouquineurs. Phyfiologie des Quais de Paris du Pont Royal au Pont Sully. Maifon Quantin. Paris 1893 Octavo.

UZANNE, OCTAVE. Les Evolutions du bou-
quin. La Nouvelle Bibliopolis. Henri Floury.
Paris 1897 Octavo.

VACARESCA, HELENE. The Bard of the
Dimbovitza. Roumanian Folk Songs collected
from the peafants by H.V., tranflated by Carmen
Sylva and Alma Strettell. Firft and fecond feries.
Two Volumes. Ofgood and Co. London 1892-
1894 Octavo.

VALE PRESS PUBLICATIONS.

BROWNING, ROBERT. Dramatic Roman-
ces & Lyrics. With border and initials defigned
and cut on the wood by Charles Ricketts. 1899
Demy Octavo. Two copies.

PERAULT, C. Deux contes de ma mère Loye.
With a frontifpiece in gold and colours and other
woodcut decorations defigned and printed by L.
Piffarro. 1899 Crown octavo. Two copies.

SHAKESPEARE, WILLIAM. The Sonnets of.
With border and decorations defigned and cut on
the wood by Charles Ricketts. 1899 Small quarto. Two copies.

SHAKESPEARE, WILLIAM. The Paffion-
ate Pilgrim & the Songs in Shakefpeare's Plays.
With decorations defigned and cut on the wood
by C. Ricketts. 1899 Crown octavo. Two copies.

SHELLEY. Lyrical Poems of. 1898 Demy Tri-
gefimo-fecundo. Two copies.

SUCKLING, SIR JOHN. The Poems of. With
border defigned and cut on the wood by Charles
Ricketts. 1899 Demy Octavo.

THE BOOK OF RUTH AND THE BOOK
OF ESTHER. 1896 Crown Duodecimo.

SYDNEY, SIR PHILIP. With border defigned
and cut on the wood by Charles Ricketts. 1899
Demy octavo.

VOGUE, EUGENE MELCHIOR DE. Le
Manteau de Jofeph Olenine. Librairie. L. Con-
quet. Paris 1889 Quarto.

WATSON, WILLIAM. The Father of the For-
eft. J. Lane. London 1895 Octavo. Large Paper.
Two copies.

WORDSWORTH, W. Poems chofen and edited by Matthew Arnold. Macmillan. London
1893. Golden Treafury Series.

LIST OF ILLUSTRATIONS.

This Catalogue was printed by S.T.
Prideaux and K. Adams in
the Spring of 1900 at 37
Norfolk Square
London

PLATES

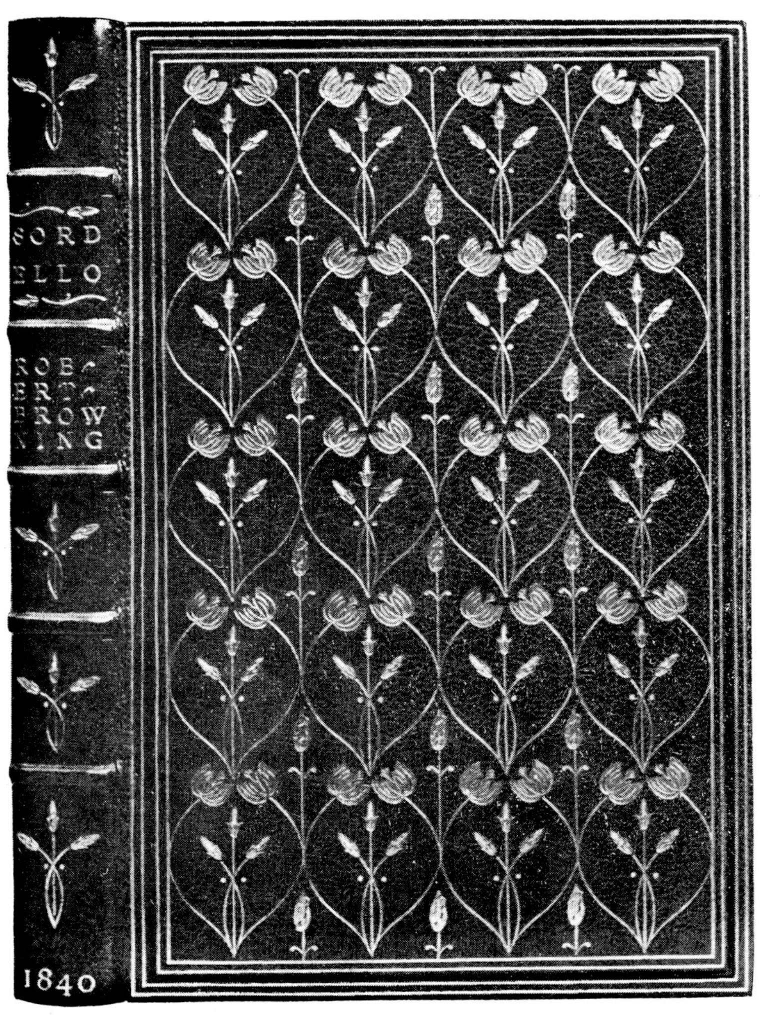

Plate 1

Plate 2

Plate 3

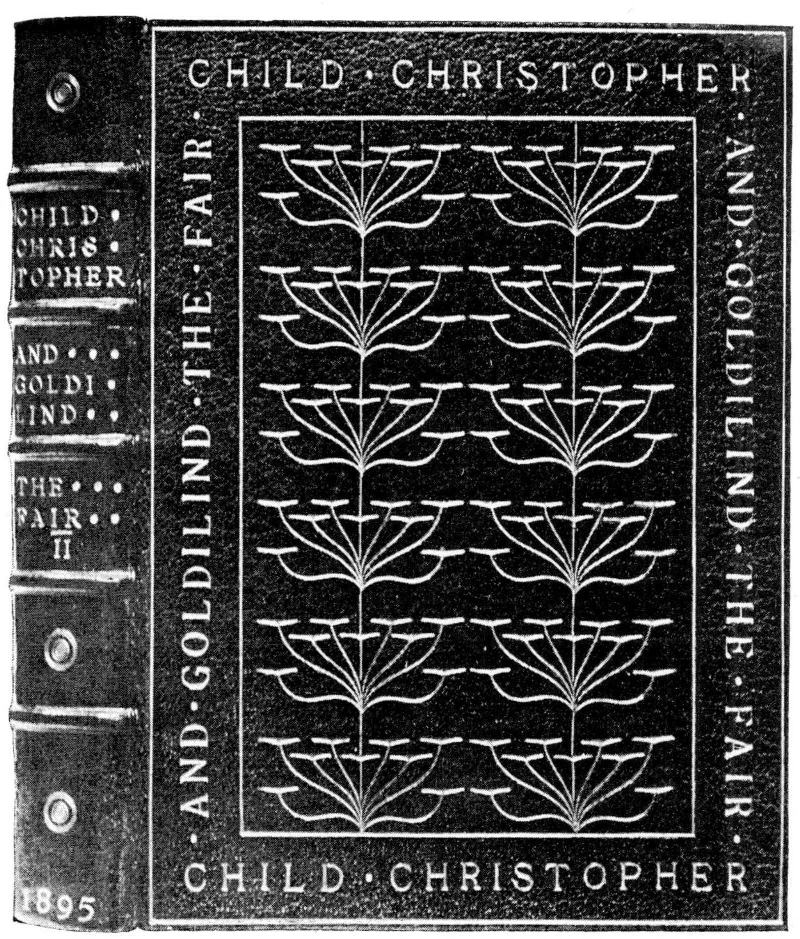

CHILD · CHRISTOPHER
AND · GOLDILIND · THE · FAIR ·
· AND · GOLDILIND · THE · FAIR ·
· GOLDILIND · THE · FAIR ·
CHILD · CHRISTOPHER
CHILD ·
CHRIS ·
TOPHER
AND · · ·
GOLDI ·
LIND · ·
THE · · ·
FAIR · ·
II
1895

Plate 4

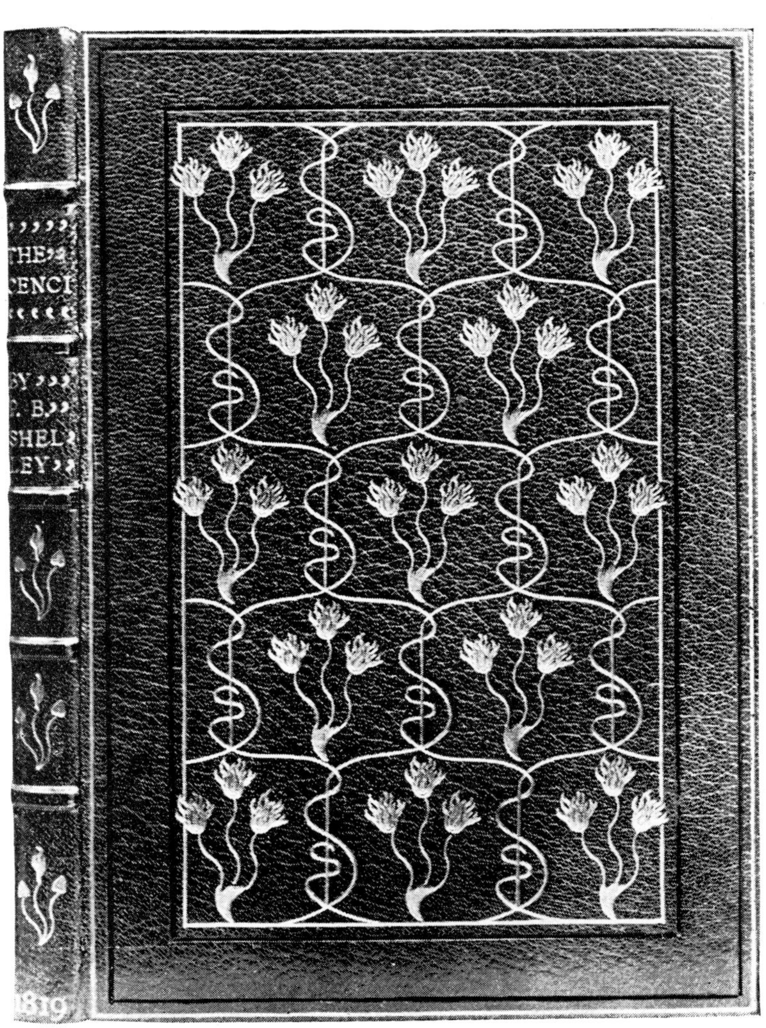

Plate 5

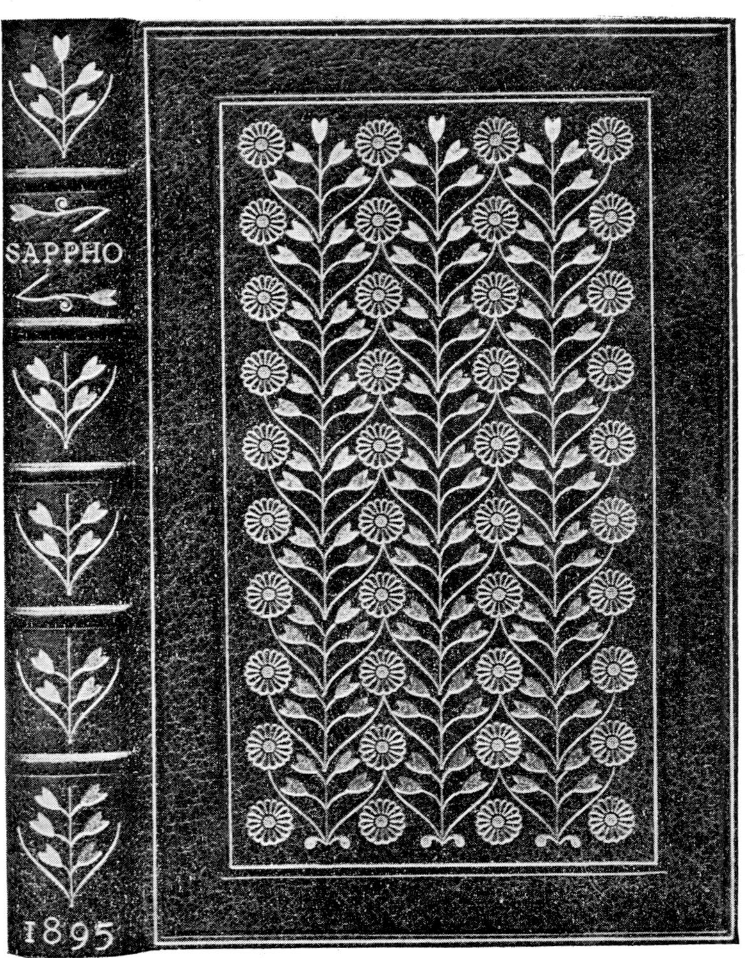

Plate 6

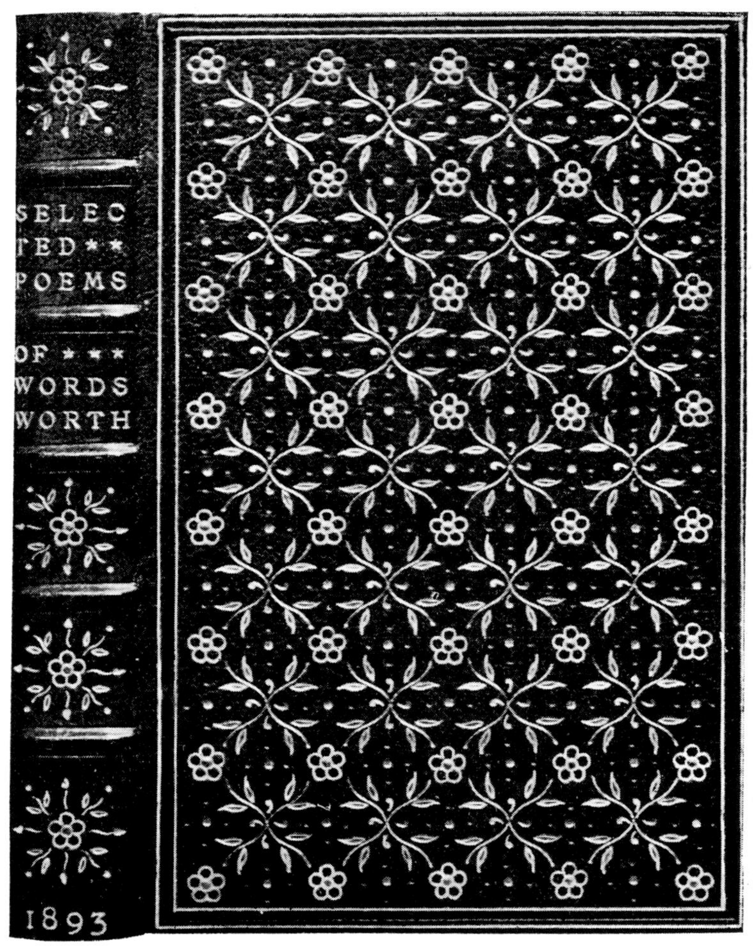

Plate 7

Plate 8

Plate 9

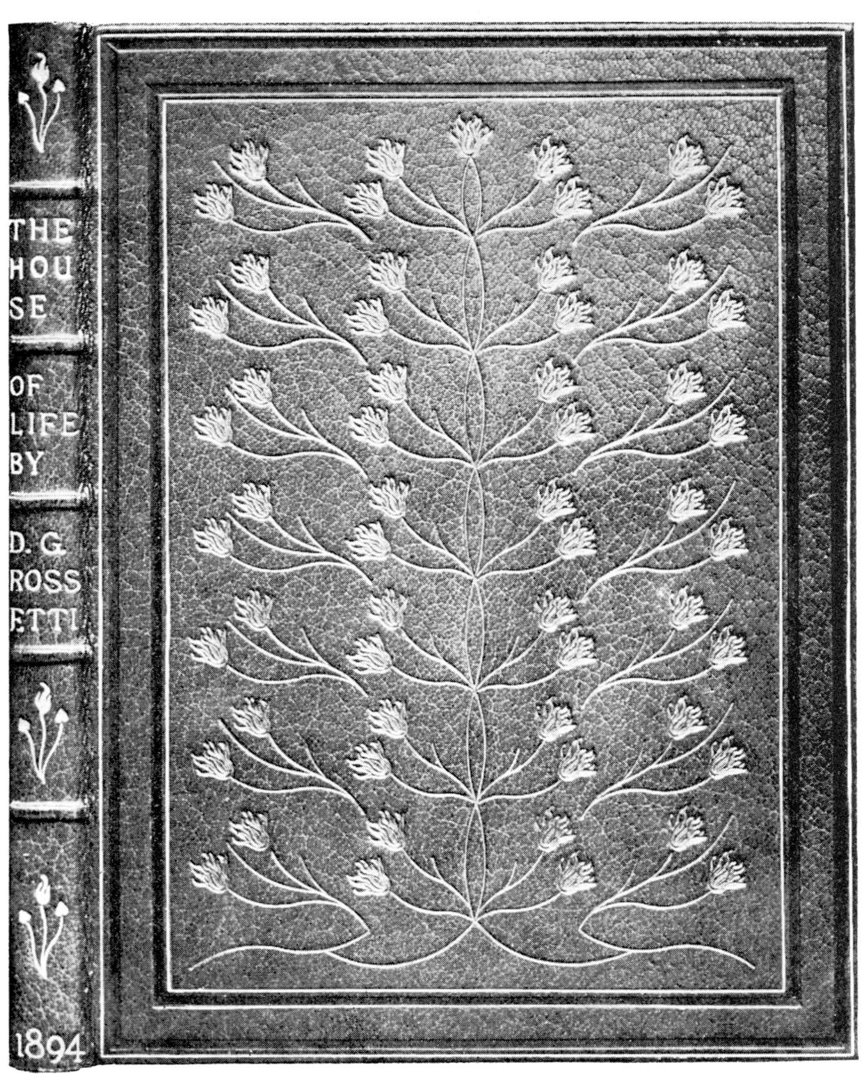

Plate 10

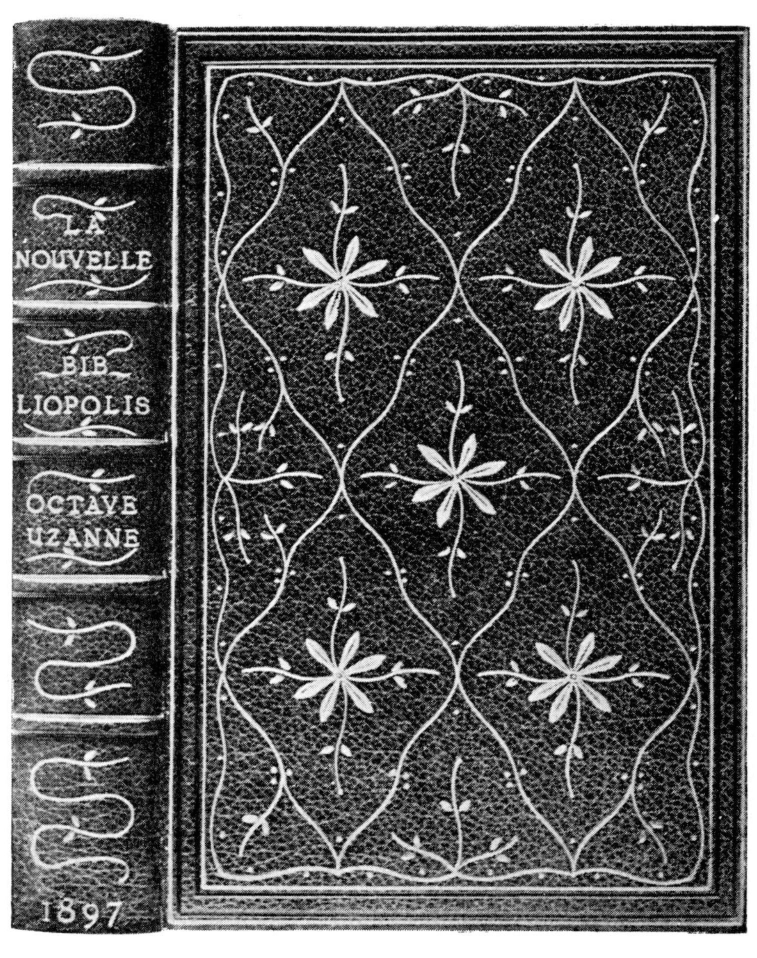

Plate 11

Plate 12

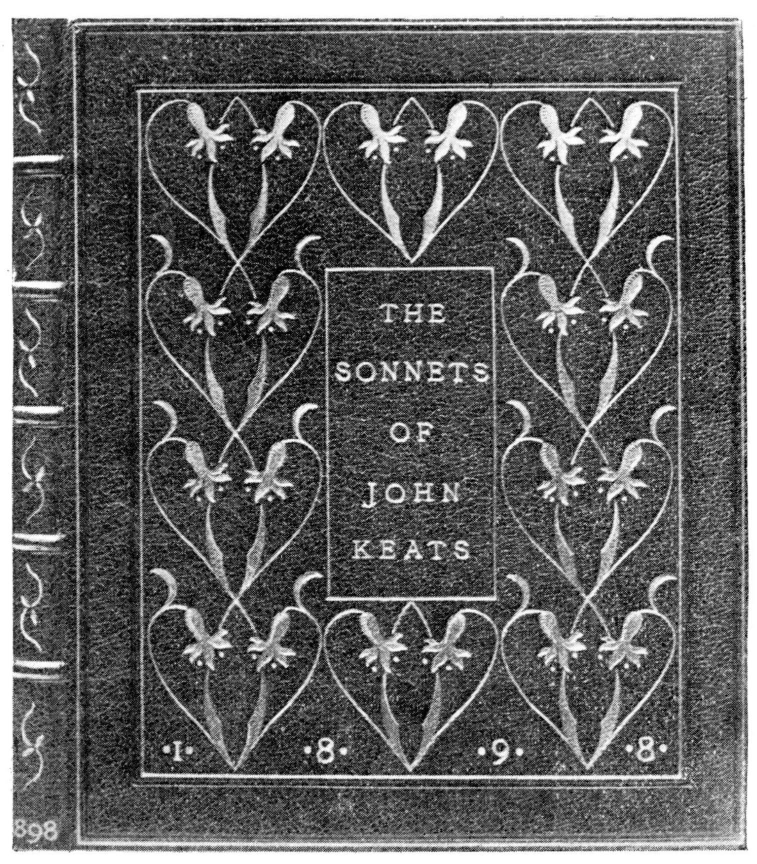

Plate 13

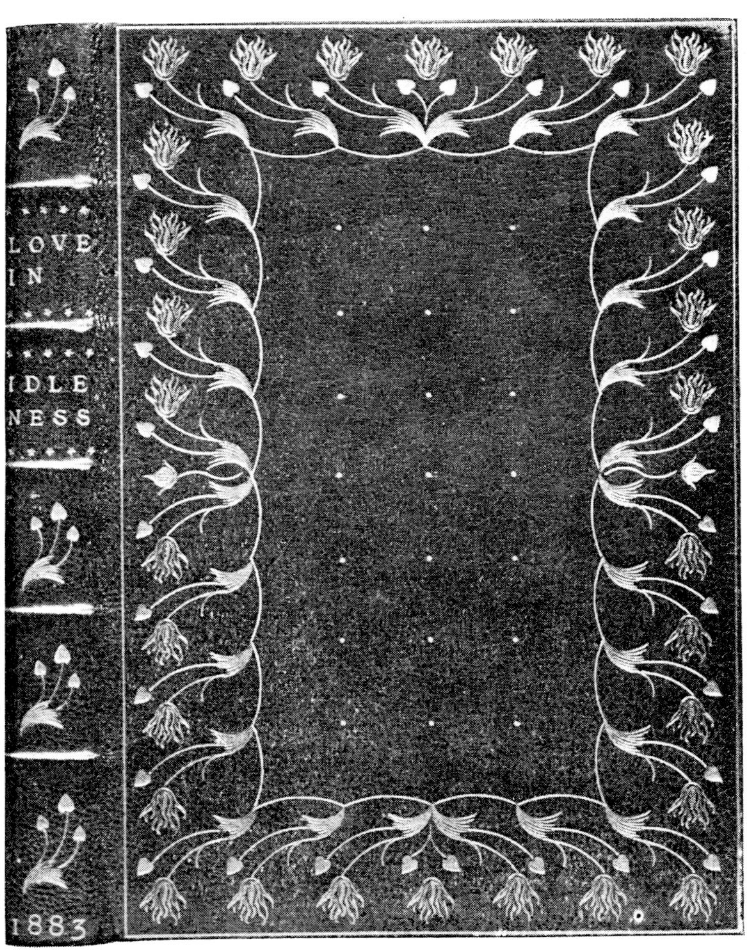

Plate 14

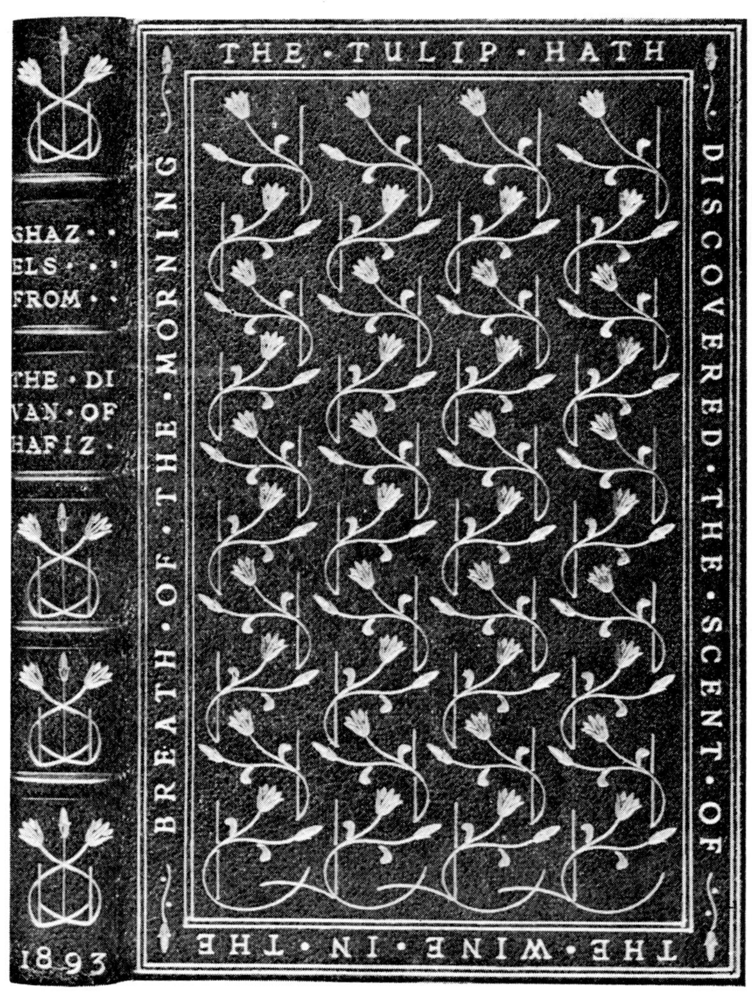

GHAZ
ELS
FROM
THE · DI
VAN · OF
HAFIZ
1893
THE · TULIP · HATH
DISCOVERED · THE · SCENT · OF
THE · WINE · IN · THE
BREATH · OF · THE · MORNING

Plate 15

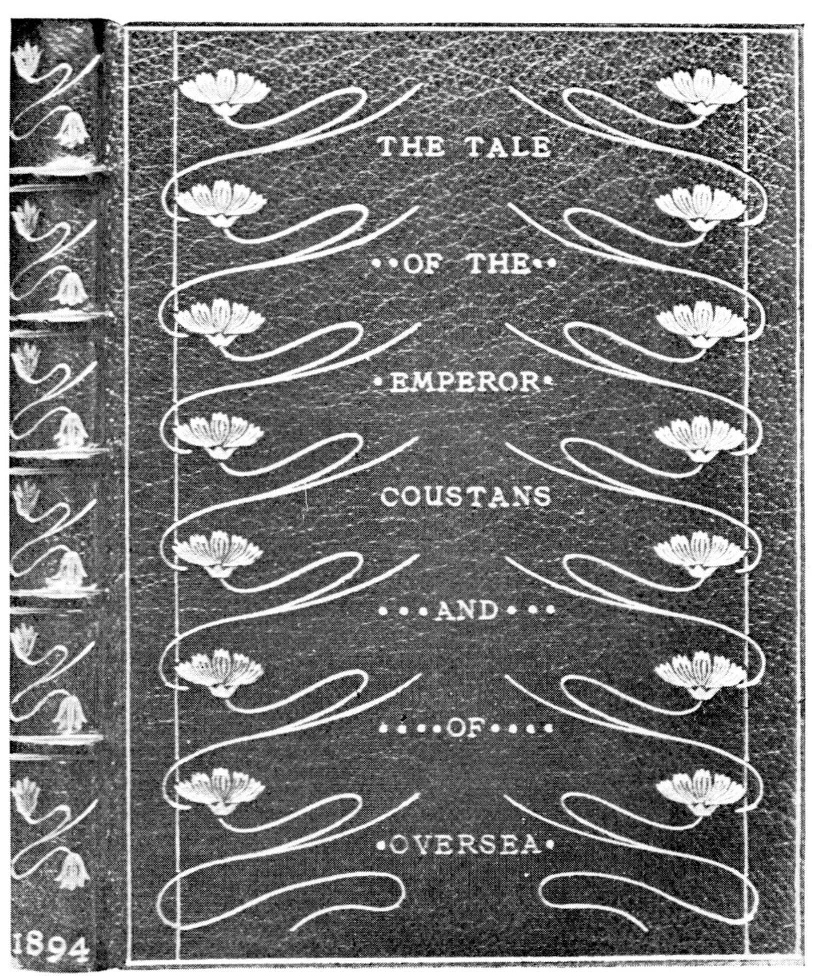

Plate 16

Plate 17

Plate 18

Plate 19

Plate 20

Plate 21

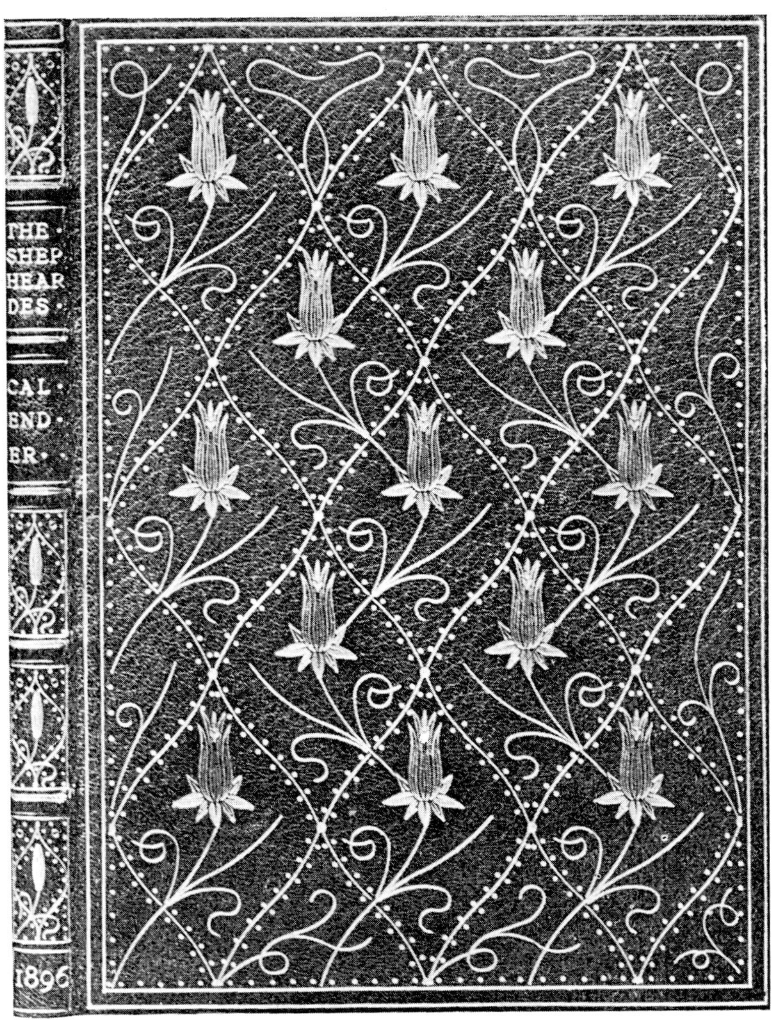

Plate 22

Plate 23

Plate 24

Plate 2 5

Plate 26